T0015026

Song of the Open Road

To know the *universe itself* as a road, as many roads, as roads for *traveling souls.*

Walt Whitman

SONG OF THE
Open Road

AMERICAN ROOTS

Applewood Books
CARLISLE, MASSACHUSETTS

978-1-4290-9638-6

"Song of the Open Road" is a part of the classic poetry collection *The Leaves of Grass*. In 1856, Walt Whitman added the poem to the second edition of the classic work as "Poem of the Road." In the 1867 edition the poem was renamed "Song of the Open Road." In the 1881 edition the poem was divided into fifteen sections.

Thank you for purchasing an Applewood book. Applewood reprints America's lively classics—books from the past that are still of interest to modern readers. Our mission is to build a picture of America's past through its primary sources.

To inquire about this edition or to request a free copy of our current catalog featuring our best-selling books, write to:

Applewood Books
P.O. Box 27
Carlisle, MA 01741

For more complete listings, visit us on the web at www.awb.com

10 9 8 7 6 5 4 3 2 1

PRINTED IN CHINA

The short works Applewood offers in its American Roots series have been selected to connect us. The books are tactile mementos of American passions by some of America's most famous writers. Each of these has meant something very personal to me.

At seventy-plus years old, I am standing toward the end of Whitman's *Open Road*. Maybe, I faintly hope, it is just the beginning, as I will someday over the next few decades step into a byway of traveling souls and then start again. Regardless, today I am looking back, marveling at the rush of people, events, and stray moments tumbling toward me. I have traveled with Walt Whitman, and I hope you travel with him, too, bravely heading up or down the road and into the unknown, embracing opportunity and change. Here is Whitman's anthem: life should be led strenuously, with passion for everyone and everything and with purpose.

"To know the universe itself as a road, as many roads, as roads for traveling souls."

                                 ❧ Phil Zuckerman
                                      PUBLISHER

1

Afoot and light-hearted I take to the
   open road,
Healthy, free, the world before me,
The long brown path before me leading
   wherever I choose.

Henceforth I ask not good-fortune, I
   myself am good-fortune,
Henceforth I whimper no more,
   postpone no more, need nothing,
Done with indoor complaints, libraries,
   querulous criticisms,
Strong and content I travel the open
   road.

The earth, that is sufficient,
I do not want the constellations any
    nearer,
I know they are very well where they
    are,
I know they suffice for those who
    belong to them.

(Still here I carry my old delicious
    burdens,
I carry them, men and women, I carry
    them with me wherever I go,
I swear it is impossible for me to get rid
    of them,
I am fill'd with them, and I will fill them
    in return.)

2

You road I enter upon and look around,
    I believe you are not all that is here,
I believe that much unseen is also here.

Here the profound lesson of reception,
    nor preference nor denial,
The black with his woolly head, the
    felon, the diseas'd, the illiterate
    person, are not denied;
The birth, the hasting after the
    physician, the beggar's tramp, the
    drunkard's stagger, the laughing
    party of mechanics,
The escaped youth, the rich person's
    carriage, the fop, the eloping couple,

The early market-man, the hearse, the
    moving of furniture into the town,
    the return back from the town,
They pass, I also pass, any thing passes,
    none can be interdicted,
None but are accepted, none but shall
    be dear to me.

3

You air that serves me with breath to
    speak!
You objects that call from diffusion my
    meanings and give them shape!
You light that wraps me and all things in
    delicate equable showers!
You paths worn in the irregular hollows
    by the roadsides!
I believe you are latent with unseen
    existences, you are so dear to me.

You flagg'd walks of the cities! you
    strong curbs at the edges!
You ferries! you planks and posts of
    wharves! you timber-lined sides! you
    distant ships!

You rows of houses! you window-pierc'd
    façades! you roofs!
You porches and entrances! you copings
    and iron guards!
You windows whose transparent shells
    might expose so much!

You doors and ascending steps! you
arches!
You gray stones of interminable
pavements! you trodden crossings!
From all that has touch'd you I believe
you have imparted to yourselves, and
now would impart the same secretly
to me,
From the living and the dead you have
peopled your impassive surfaces, and
the spirits thereof would be evident
and amicable with me.

4

The earth expanding right hand and left
hand,
The picture alive, every part in its best
light,
The music falling in where it is wanted,
and stopping where it is not wanted,
The cheerful voice of the public road,
the gay fresh sentiment of the road.

O highway I travel, do you say to me Do
    not leave me?
Do you say Venture not—if you leave
    me you are lost?
Do you say I am already prepared, I am
    well-beaten and undenied, adhere to
    me?

O public road, I say back I am not afraid
    to leave you, yet I love you,
You express me better than I can express
    myself,
You shall be more to me than my poem.

I think heroic deeds were all conceiv'd
    in the open air, and all free poems
    also,
I think I could stop here myself and do
    miracles,
I think whatever I shall meet on the
    road I shall like, and whoever
    beholds me shall like me,
I think whoever I see must be happy.

5

From this hour I ordain myself loos'd of
    limits and imaginary lines,
Going where I list, my own master total
    and absolute,
Listening to others, considering well
    what they say,
Pausing, searching, receiving,
    contemplating,
Gently, but with undeniable will,
    divesting myself of the holds that
    would hold me.
I inhale great draughts of space,
The east and the west are mine, and the
    north and the south are mine.

I am larger, better than I thought,
I did not know I held so much goodness.

All seems beautiful to me,
I can repeat over to men and women
    You have done such good to me I
    would do the same to you,

I will recruit for myself and you as I go,
I will scatter myself among men and
    women as I go,
I will toss a new gladness and roughness
    among them,
Whoever denies me it shall not trouble
    me,
Whoever accepts me he or she shall be
    blessed and shall bless me.

6

Now if a thousand perfect men were to
    appear it would not amaze me,
Now if a thousand beautiful forms
    of women appear'd it would not
    astonish me.

Now I see the secret of the making of
    the best persons,
It is to grow in the open air and to eat
    and sleep with the earth.

Here a great personal deed has room,
(Such a deed seizes upon the hearts of
    the whole race of men,
Its effusion of strength and will
    overwhelms law and mocks all
    authority and all argument against
    it.)

Here is the test of wisdom,
Wisdom is not finally tested in schools,
Wisdom cannot be pass'd from one
    having it to another not having it,
Wisdom is of the soul, is not susceptible
    of proof, is its own proof,
Applies to all stages and objects and
    qualities and is content,
Is the certainty of the reality and
    immortality of things, and the
    excellence of things;
Something there is in the float of the
    sight of things that provokes it out
    of the soul.

Now I re-examine philosophies and
    religions,
They may prove well in lecture-
    rooms, yet not prove at all under
    the spacious clouds and along the
    landscape and flowing currents.

Here is realization,
Here is a man tallied—he realizes here
    what he has in him,
The past, the future, majesty, love—if
    they are vacant of you, you are
    vacant of them.

Only the kernel of every object
    nourishes;
Where is he who tears off the husks for
    you and me?
Where is he that undoes stratagems and
    envelopes for you and me?

Here is adhesiveness, it is not previously
    fashion'd, it is apropos;

Do you know what it is as you pass to
    be loved by strangers?
Do you know the talk of those turning
    eye-balls?

7

Here is the efflux of the soul,
The efflux of the soul comes from
    within through embower'd gates,
    ever provoking questions,
These yearnings why are they? these
    thoughts in the darkness why are
    they?
Why are there men and women that
    while they are nigh me the sunlight
    expands my blood?
Why when they leave me do my
    pennants of joy sink flat and lank?
Why are there trees I never walk under
    but large and melodious thoughts
    descend upon me?

(I think they hang there winter and
      summer on those trees and always
      drop fruit as I pass;)
What is it I interchange so suddenly
      with strangers?
What with some driver as I ride on the
      seat by his side?
What with some fisherman drawing his
      seine by the shore as I walk by and
      pause?
What gives me to be free to a woman's
      and man's good-will? what gives
      them to be free to mine?

8

The efflux of the soul is happiness, here
      is happiness,
I think it pervades the open air, waiting
      at all times,
Now it flows unto us, we are rightly
      charged.

Here rises the fluid and attaching
    character,
The fluid and attaching character is the
    freshness and sweetness of man and
    woman,
(The herbs of the morning sprout no
    fresher and sweeter every day out
    of the roots of themselves, than it
    sprouts fresh and sweet continually
    out of itself.)

Toward the fluid and attaching
    character exudes the sweat of the
    love of young and old,
From it falls distill'd the charm that
    mocks beauty and attainments,
Toward it heaves the shuddering
    longing ache of contact.

9

Allons! whoever you are come travel
      with me!
Traveling with me you find what never
      tires.

The earth never tires,
The earth is rude, silent,
      incomprehensible at first, Nature is
      rude and incomprehensible at first,
Be not discouraged, keep on, there are
      divine things well envelop'd,
I swear to you there are divine things
      more beautiful than words can tell.

Allons! we must not stop here,
However sweet these laid-up stores,
      however convenient this dwelling
      we cannot remain here,
However shelter'd this port and
      however calm these waters we must
      not anchor here,

However welcome the hospitality that
    surrounds us we are permitted to
    receive it but a little while.

10

Allons! the inducements shall be greater,
We will sail pathless and wild seas,
We will go where winds blow, waves
    dash, and the Yankee clipper speeds
    by under full sail.

Allons! with power, liberty, the earth,
    the elements,
Health, defiance, gayety, self-esteem,
    curiosity;
Allons! from all formules!
From your formules, O bat-eyed and
    materialistic priests.

The stale cadaver blocks up the
    passage—the burial waits no longer.

Allons! yet take warning!
He traveling with me needs the best
    blood, thews, endurance,
None may come to the trial till he or she
    bring courage and health,
Come not here if you have already spent
    the best of yourself,
Only those may come who come in
    sweet and determin'd bodies,
No diseas'd person, no rum-drinker or
    venereal taint is permitted here.

(I and mine do not convince by
    arguments, similes, rhymes,
We convince by our presence.)

11

Listen! I will be honest with you,
I do not offer the old smooth prizes, but
    offer rough new prizes,
These are the days that must happen to
    you:

You shall not heap up what is call'd
  riches,
You shall scatter with lavish hand all
  that you earn or achieve,
You but arrive at the city to which you
  were destin'd, you hardly settle
  yourself to satisfaction before you
  are call'd by an irresistible call to
  depart,
You shall be treated to the ironical
  smiles and mockings of those who
  remain behind you,
What beckonings of love you receive
  you shall only answer with
  passionate kisses of parting,
You shall not allow the hold of those
  who spread their reach'd hands
  toward you.

12

Allons! after the great Companions, and
    to belong to them!
They too are on the road—they are the
    swift and majestic men—they are
    the greatest women,
Enjoyers of calms of seas and storms of
    seas,
Sailors of many a ship, walkers of many
    a mile of land,
Habituès of many distant countries,
    habituès of far-distant dwellings,
Trusters of men and women, observers
    of cities, solitary toilers,
Pausers and contemplators of tufts,
    blossoms, shells of the shore,
Dancers at wedding-dances, kissers of
    brides, tender helpers of children,
    bearers of children,
Soldiers of revolts, standers by gaping
    graves, lowerers-down of coffins,

Journeyers over consecutive seasons,
    over the years, the curious years
    each emerging from that which
    preceded it,
Journeyers as with companions, namely
    their own diverse phases,
Forth-steppers from the latent
    unrealized baby-days,
Journeyers gayly with their own youth,
    journeyers with their bearded and
    well-grain'd manhood,
Journeyers with their womanhood,
    ample, unsurpass'd, content,
Journeyers with their own sublime old
    age of manhood or womanhood,
Old age, calm, expanded, broad with
    the haughty breadth of the universe,
Old age, flowing free with the delicious
    near-by freedom of death.

13

Allons! to that which is endless as it was
    beginningless,
To undergo much, tramps of days, rests
    of nights,
To merge all in the travel they tend to,
    and the days and nights they tend to,
Again to merge them in the start of
    superior journeys,
To see nothing anywhere but what you
    may reach it and pass it,
To conceive no time, however distant,
    but what you may reach it and pass
    it,
To look up or down no road but it
    stretches and waits for you, however
    long but it stretches and waits for
    you,
To see no being, not God's or any, but
    you also go thither,
To see no possession but you may
    possess it, enjoying all without labor
    or purchase, abstracting the feast yet
    not abstracting one particle of it,

To take the best of the farmer's farm and
    the rich man's elegant villa, and the
    chaste blessings of the well-married
    couple, and the fruits of orchards
    and flowers of gardens,
To take to your use out of the compact
    cities as you pass through,
To carry buildings and streets with you
    afterward wherever you go,
To gather the minds of men out of their
    brains as you encounter them, to
    gather the love out of their hearts,
To take your lovers on the road with
    you, for all that you leave them
    behind you,
To know the universe itself as a road, as
    many roads, as roads for traveling
    souls.

All parts away for the progress of souls,
All religion, all solid things, arts,
    governments—all that was or is
    apparent upon this globe or any
    globe, falls into niches and corners

before the procession of souls along
the grand roads of the universe.

Of the progress of the souls of men and
women along the grand roads of the
universe, all other progress is the
needed emblem and sustenance.

Forever alive, forever forward,
Stately, solemn, sad, withdrawn, baffled,
mad, turbulent, feeble, dissatisfied,
Desperate, proud, fond, sick, accepted
by men, rejected by men,
They go! they go! I know that they go,
but I know not where they go,
But I know that they go toward the
best—toward something great.

Whoever you are, come forth! or man or
woman come forth!
You must not stay sleeping and dallying
there in the house, though you built
it, or though it has been built for
you.

Out of the dark confinement! out from
    behind the screen!
It is useless to protest, I know all and
    expose it.

Behold through you as bad as the rest,
Through the laughter, dancing, dining,
    supping, of people,
Inside of dresses and ornaments, inside
    of those wash'd and trimm'd faces,
Behold a secret silent loathing and
    despair.

No husband, no wife, no friend, trusted
    to hear the confession,
Another self, a duplicate of every one,
    skulking and hiding it goes,
Formless and wordless through the
    streets of the cities, polite and bland
    in the parlors,
In the cars of railroads, in steamboats, in
    the public assembly,

Home to the houses of men and
    women, at the table, in the bedroom,
    everywhere,
Smartly attired, countenance smiling,
    form upright, death under the breast-
    bones, hell under the skull-bones,
Under the broadcloth and gloves, under
    the ribbons and artificial flowers,
Keeping fair with the customs, speaking
    not a syllable of itself,
Speaking of any thing else but never of
    itself.

14

Allons! through struggles and wars!
The goal that was named cannot be
    countermanded.

Have the past struggles succeeded?
What has succeeded? yourself? your
    nation? Nature?

Now understand me well—it is
    provided in the essence of things
    that from any fruition of success,
    no matter what, shall come forth
    something to make a greater struggle
    necessary.

My call is the call of battle, I nourish
    active rebellion,
He going with me must go well arm'd,
He going with me goes often with
    spare diet, poverty, angry enemies,
    desertions.

15

Allons! the road is before us!
It is safe—I have tried it—my own feet
    have tried it well—be not detain'd!

Let the paper remain on the desk
    unwritten, and the book on the shelf
    unopen'd!

Let the tools remain in the workshop!
    let the money remain unearn'd!
Let the school stand! mind not the cry
    of the teacher!
Let the preacher preach in his pulpit!
    let the lawyer plead in the court, and
    the judge expound the law.

Camerado, I give you my hand!
I give you my love more precious than
    money,
I give you myself before preaching or
    law;
Will you give me yourself? will you
    come travel with me?
Shall we stick by each other as long as
    we live?